THE WINTER COUNT

The Winter Count

Dilys Leman

McGill-Queen's University Press

Montreal & Kingston • London • Ithaca

ISBN 978-0-7735-4413-0 (paper)
ISBN 978-0-7735-9639-9 (ePDF)
ISBN 978-0-7735-9640-5 (ePUB)

Legal deposit third quarter 2014
Bibliothèque nationale du Québec

Printed in Canada on acid-free paper that is 100% ancient forest
free (100% post-consumer recycled), processed chlorine free

McGill-Queen's University Press acknowledges the support
of the Canada Council for the Arts for our publishing
program. We also acknowledge the financial support of the
Government of Canada through the Canada Book Fund
for our publishing activities.

Library and Archives Canada Cataloguing in Publication

Leman, Dilys, 1954–, author
  The winter count / Dilys Leman.

  (The Hugh MacLennan poetry series)
  Poems.
  Issued in print and electronic formats.
  ISBN 978-0-7735-4413-0 (pbk.). –
  ISBN 978-0-7735-9639-9 (ePDF). –
  ISBN 978-0-7735-9640-5 (ePUB)

  1. Native peoples – Canada – Government relations –
Poetry. 2. Riel, Louis, 1844–1885 – Mental health –
Poetry. I. Title. II. Series: Hugh MacLennan poetry series

PS8623.E5324W55 2014   C811'.6   C2014-902916-0
                                       C2014-902917-9

This book was typeset by Interscript in 9.5/13 New Baskerville.

CONTENTS

THE WINTER COUNT

*The Indians are quick at discovering the worth of a man
into whose company they are thrown.*

Dr Augustus Jukes, 1886

Marinade for Factory Drive-Belts

Take several thousand
bison carcasses and lightly
marinade with strychnine.

Yield for one 2,000-pounder:
20 wolf pelts and assorted
pelt dishes – coyotes, foxes,
magpies, Indian dogs.

Quick results.
No bullet holes.

Helpful Hint #1

Bison leathers make
the sturdiest drive-belts
for the factory machines.

Helpful Hint #2

To feed large parties
of railway crews and land
surveyors, take one bison
carcass (omit strychnine).
Slice thinly and dry over
a slow fire until brittle.

Pound into powder-like
bits. Mix with suet and seasonal
berries. Properly stored,
this nutritious treat keeps
indefinitely.

Rot-gut Whiskey

Take one gallon of pure
grain alcohol. Cut with water.

Add tobacco, red ink, a dash
of Jamaica ginger (to taste).

Strychnine optional.

Potluck Surprise, 1873

In Cypress Hills bowl
combine four trading posts
employing mostly American
rot-gut traders and bison-robe
hunters. Add 10 Métis freighters
with oxen and carts.

Gradually stir in 300
Assiniboine camped near
Solomon's and Farwell's
whiskey forts.

Fold in two American wolfers
ranting about 40 missing horses.
Add four heaping tablespoons
of preserved suppositions.
Season liberally and let stand
until thickened.

Add two to three festive
kegs and taste for drunken:
Indians, wolfers, traders
Métis, etc.

Whisk in one missing
horse and several irate
wolfers until batter
stiffens. Place Assiniboine
in centre of well-greased pan.

Arrange wolfers, whiskey-
traders and Métis freighters
in protective coulee along
sides of pan. With repeating
rifles (Winchesters and Henrys)
volley rapidly into camp.

Shoot the fleeing. Burn lodges.
Rape women. Execute
the wounded. Bake in hot oven
until 25 Assiniboine are dead
(women and children included).

Using a clean, sharp
knife, test for survivors.

NEW RECRUIT

Oath of Office

I solemnly swear that
I will faithfully
diligently and
impartially

execute and
perform the duties
required of me
as a member of the
North-West Mounted Police

and will well and truly
obey and perform
all lawful orders and
instructions which I shall
receive as such

without fear
favour or
affection of
or towards
any person
or party
whomsoever

So help me God.

Articles issued on joining, to be kept in serviceable condition at the Constable's expense during his whole term of service:

Buffalo Robe 1
Blankets .... 2 pair
Waterproof Sheet 1
Buffalo Coat 1
Cloth Overcoat 1
Helmet 1
Fur Cap 1
Gauntlets, Buckskin .... 1 pair
Drawers, Woollen .... 2 "
Undershirts, Woollen 2
Overshirts, Flannel 2
Socks, Woollen .... 4 pair
Stockings, Woollen .... 2 "
Mitts, Woollen .... 1 "
Spurs .... 1 "
Towels 2
Kit Bag 1
Haversack 1
Moccasins .... 1 pair
Holdall 1
Knife 1
Fork 1
Spoon 1
Razor and Case 1
Comb 1
Shaving Brush 1
Blacking " 1

Polishing " 1
Cloth " 1
Button " 1
" Brass 1
Sponge 1
Burnisher 1
Cup 1
Saucer 1
Plate 1

Articles issued annually, to be kept in serviceable condition
at the Constable's expense:

Forage Cap 1
Tunic, Serge 1
Jacket, Stable 1
Breeches, Cloth .... 2 pair
Trousers, Stable .... 1 "
Boots, Long .... 1 "
" Short .... 1 "

One Scarlet Tunic

    will be issued
    to each Constable
        on joining,

    and another
    during his
        third year
    of service.

On First Patrol

Blanket socks overshirt brush
button gauntlets comb
      knife   she took from me
      stripped meat   fresh kill   chewed
          deposited on tongue
            gagging throat
        Swallow s*hhhh*   *drink this*

she is Cree
      I think   fireflies for eyes
    sweetgrass burning   or is it sage
   see the two suns?   two haloed suns
       and insects thrumming underground
         conspiracy   *shhhhh drink*
       fingers temples   pulling the heat   pulling
   the brass buttons   my scarlet tunic my
scarlet tunic   possibilities
      death shroud   baby carrier
      death shroud

what to bargain for
         shhh   drink this
     one pair boots for one
       good rain
         one good horse for fifty miles

one carbine   a single ball   one open mouth

IT IS THE DESIRE OF HER MAJESTY TO OPEN UP

From Treaty Four, 1874, Fort Qu'Appelle, Saskatchewan

for settlement immigration trade a tract
of country bounded and described as hereinafter
consent thereto of Her Indian subjects assured
of Her bounty and benevolence name certain Chiefs
and Headmen authorized to sign do hereby cede
release surrender yield up all rights titles privileges
whatsoever forever assign reserves one square mile
each family of five in token of good behaviour
each Chief a coat a Queen's silver medal a census
to be taken annually paid in cash each Chief twenty-
five dollars each Headman fifteen every other Indian
five dollars per head the following articles supplied
to any band cultivating the soil or hereafter two hoes
one spade one scythe one axe and for every family
enough seed wheat barley oats potatoes to plant
such land as broken up one plough two harrows
for every ten families each Chief for the use of his
band one yoke of oxen one bull four cows a chest
of ordinary carpenter's tools five hand saws five
augers one cross-cut saw one pit-saw the necessary
files and grindstone aforesaid articles to be given
once for all a school a teacher no intoxicating
liquor said Indians shall have right to pursue
avocations of hunting trapping fishing throughout
the tract surrendered subject to regulations required
for settlement mining lumbering other purposes

the undersigned Chiefs and Headman do hereby
solemnly promise and engage obey abide maintain
peace and good order in witness whereof Her
Majesty's said Commissioners and the said Indian
Chiefs and Headmen have here unto subscribed
and set their hands

ALEXANDER MORRIS   X   KA-KII-SHI-WAY   X   PIS-QUA
DAVID LAIR   X   KA-WEZ-ANCE   X   KA-KEE-NA-WUP
WILLIAM J. CHRISTIE   X   KUS-KEE-TEW-MUS-COO-MUSQUA
KA-NE-ON-US-KA-TEW   X   CAN-AH-HA-CHA-PEW
KII-SI-CAW-CHUCK   X   KA-RA-CA-TOOSE
KA-KII-NIS-TA-HAW   X   CHA-CA-CHAS
WA-PII-MOOSE-TOO-SUS   X   MEEMAY

Each Chief shall receive hereafter in recognition
of the closing of the treaty a suitable flag.

Augustus Jukes (Glenbow Archives / NA-2788-94)

A MORE SUITABLE PROTECTION

Augustus Jukes

For the organs of generation,
when riding in severe weather,

and long since adopted
throughout these Territories,

      is a small piece of softly draped rabbit skin

to be applied, not *with* the skin,
but *outside* the shirt and drawers,

removed in a moment
when no longer required.

Leave wife and seven children
and head west, to the Saskatchewan

Choose 640 acres in the Touchwood Hills

Dwell in a leaking government-issue
tent while you await the tools

you will need to build the Home
Farm house. Ignore persistent

chest pains. Decide whether to live
in the granary during winter

Build the granary

Hire Indians to haul the timbers
Teach them to do the very hard

work of pit-sawing, and to cut
and prepare the fence rails

Pay them in rations of flour and tea
in accordance with regulations

When your provisions are almost
depleted, issue Indian Department

pork – musty and rusty, each portion
calculated in Ottawa as sufficient

At your own expense, provide blankets
and moose skins for the colder days

Do not pester the Department about
your application for a warm big-chested
Clydesdale

*

Walk to the reserves. Estimate the acreage
not entirely swampy and tree-covered

Examine their agricultural tools. Compile
a list of ploughs and harrows issued

incomplete – wanting rods, bolts, clevis
doubletrees, whiffletrees

Demonstrate techniques appropriate
to *prairie* (dry land) farming conditions:

Turn the sod in shallow furrows
Plough again at a deeper level

Wait until the following spring
to sow. (Find a calm interpreter

to explain the repercussions
of late spring run-offs and early
frost on fields of wheat)

Foster a spirit of making do, making
the best of inferior seed or no seed

Of freight oxen ill-disposed to the plough

Weak sore-footed Montana milk cows
that perish in winter

Promote acts of virtuous peasant labour
(know that mechanical reapers, threshers
and binders will be unauthorized for Indian use)

Collect samples from rot-infested potato fields

Celebrate the first wheat crop, the first
live-birth calf in spring

Ask the interpreter to explain why
all livestock and implements are considered

the property of the government

surplus crops to be stored in a central
depot and held subject to the order
of the Indian Agent for the District

Trust in Her Majesty's bounty and benevolence

Count the children

Intoxicating
  liquors
  and other intoxicants

are prohibited
to be manufactured
or made
  in the said
  North-West Territories

except by
  special permission
  of the Governor of Council

or to be imported
  or brought into the same
  from any Province of Canada
  or elsewhere

or to be sold
  exchanged
  traded
  or bartered

except by
> special permission
> in writing
>
> of the Lieutenant-Governor
> of the said Territories

IT IS THE DESIRE OF HER MAJESTY TO FEED

From Treaty Six, 1876, Forts Carlton and Pitt, Saskatchewan

That in the event hereafter
of the Indians comprised
within this treaty being

> *Weekaskookwasayin*
> *(Chief Sweet Grass):*

overtaken by any pestilence
or by a general famine

> *"You heard them say it –*

the Queen, on being satisfied
and certified

> *the Grandmother has*

thereof by her Indian Agent
or Agents will grant to the Indians

> *very   big   breasts*

assistance of such character
and to such extent as

> *She'll feed us*

Her Chief Superintendent
of Indian Affairs shall deem

if

necessary and sufficient

starvation comes. "

Hunters shooting bison from a railway train. *Harper's Weekly*, 2 August 1884 (Glenbow Archives / NA-1406-188)

WORDS FOR BUFFALO

Augustus Jukes

buffel (Middle French)
bufalo (Portugese)

bufalus (Latin variant of
bubalus, from Greek

boubalos) – originally a kind
of African antelope

and later – a type
of domesticated ox
in southern Asia
and the Mediterranean

Wrongfully applied
to the North American
bison (from French and Latin)

Iinnii (in Blackfoot)
Otapanihowin (in Cree)

A GRANDER CALLING: EXPLANATIONS AT TEA

Phoebe Jukes

He was for many years
among the most respected

men of St Catharines,
but with the depression

of 1875, he made himself
responsible for others,

dispensing loans like lollipops,
the door to his office open

to any patient unable to pay.
It became impossible for him

to collect the accounts. Impossible
to re-pay the debts incurred

when he permitted himself to be
considered as a member of Parliament,

then lost to that lying, lily-lipped
Liberal. Oh, the effrontery of that

protracted contest! It allowed
(in his absence) carrion crows –

inconceivably foul and uncongenial –
to gorge upon his medical practice,

thereby prompting many ignorant
well-intentioned friends to suggest

he seek refuge in a new government
appointment in the great North-West.

And he, I suppose, envisioned the role
of Senior Surgeon to be proof of his

usefulness. Trust in his competence.

ON CONDITIONS IN CYPRESS HILLS

Augustus Jukes, 17 October 1882

Sir Edgar Dewdney,

There are now encamped in the immediate
vicinity of Fort Walsh, about two thousand

destitute. Some were represented to me as
absolutely starving. It would be difficult

to exaggerate their extreme wretchedness
and need. The disappearance of the buffalo

has left them without food, robes, or moccasins.
Few lodges are of buffalo hide, the majority

of cotton only, many rotten and dilapidated
a few consisting only of branches

laid upon the lodge poles. The extreme
scarcity of robes or other covering

at night is painfully apparent. At this advanced
wintry season a return to their reservations

would be impossible. For the same reason
those who are now willing to accept

the Treaty must for the present remain.
I have no hesitation in declaring my belief

that unless speedy and adequate measures
are taken to provide these suffering

people with the common necessaries of life
the result will be disastrous and even appalling.

My Dear Dewdney,

Of course they have asked again
to have reservations here

and say they may as well starve to death
here as on the reservations North and East.

But limited rations, absence of game,
scarcity of clothing, and the suffering

they must endure this winter
will I hope bring them to their senses.

INDIAN ACT 1876,
CHAPTER 18, SECTION 12

The term "person"
means an individual

other than an Indian

unless the context clearly
requires another

construction

Native grave near Eastend detachment, Saskatchewan. Sergeant G. Rolph at left (Glenbow Archives / NA-936-36)

IN WITNESS WHEREOF
Allan MacDonald Esquire
Indian Agent and the said

Big Bear Chief of the said
Band hereby giving
his adhesion to

the said treaty
have hereunto
subscribed
and set
their
hands

ALLAN MACDONALD

X BIG BEAR

A.G. IRVINE

X PIAPOT

AUGUSTUS JUKES

X JOE TANNER

JOHN COTTON

PETER HOURIE

A. SHURTLIFF

X LOUIS LEVEILLEE

W.R. ABBOTT

W. ROUTLEDGE

FRANK NORMAN

THE SOUTH SASKATCHEWAN RIVER
WILL NOT RECEDE

Unless you submit the proper request form

in quadruplet and deliver eight months

premature your report on silver spoons

sprouting between the rows of radishes

and government pledges to protect

your eyes each time you slice off pieces

of your arse with a government-issued

paring knife shaped to an Indian's

turning back

BIG BEAR'S SPEECH

Police Informant, August 1884

He said he speaks for his band
as a Chief speaks for his People

He said the White agent isn't like that –

there is always someone higher
whom he never sees

He said the Governor called upon
the Great Spirit

He said the Governor understood
that the land is only borrowed

He said he is trying to grasp the promises
He said he sees his hand closing again

and again, but he can find nothing in it

He said he is afraid to take a reserve
He said what he sees is

the tiny piece of land
he is told he must choose

He said he feels choked

He said they must speak
to that White   *than whom*
                          there is none higher

He said he does not believe
the Queen wants them to die

the way they are

He said he feels the rope around his neck

He said it sometimes comes to him
that they have been breathed over

He said it is like the trance that falls
upon them when Windigo is coming

He said they must make one Grand Council

He said they must speak with one thundering voice

THREE CLASSES OF HALF-BREEDS
IN THE TERRITORIES

Alexander Morris, 1876

1st, those who

have their farms
and homes
(will, of course,
be recognized

as at St Laurent, near Prince
Albert, the Qu'Appelle Lakes
and Edmonton,

as possessors
of the soil)

2nd, those who are
with the Indians

(have been recognized
and have passed

entirely identified
living with them and speaking
their language and
as Indians
into the bands)

3rd, those who
of French descent –
of Métis who live

do not farm, are chiefly
a large class
by the hunt of the buffalo
and have no settled
homes

(The position

of the third class
is more difficult)

WHY A CLAIRVOYANT BORDER COLLIE IS NOT ENOUGH

Phoebe Jukes

There is no shortage of men in uniform
these days. Wool gathers in a mother's mouth

when a Mountie comes to call, love
letters penned in secret railway code

stashed in his shiny boots. All good mothers
read the *Regina Leader*, its daily tally:

> *Private Alex Young, slight flesh wound in the thigh*
>
> *F. Hokes, run over by gun carriage*
>
> *William Keppen, shot through the head, killed instantly,
> the ball entering his mouth*

*

Today, I am knitting something shapeless
and undecided. Clara will show the way:

Wool-in-jaw, she races through the parlour
snaring chair legs, two tables, a potted plant.

Wool-in-mouth drop onto the man's shiny boots.
Oh dear, Mr Sanders. How to untangle without unravelling?

And he does, expertly, even as he recites
(in a single, manly breath) his favourite

harrowing tale: *Cypress Hills blizzard*
horse bad leg wolves low on rations fever 104.

The fairer sex, evidently, is prone to displays
of emotional excess in times of stress –

spontaneous, prodigious shedding of hair
on the gentleman's blue breeches. Unseemly

growling when he mentions (again) that Appaloosa
filly he rescued, her significant breeding

potential. Roll over, Clara! Play dead when
that daughter of mine recites another love

poem of Hafiz, wedding dresses gathering in her
eyes like great white flocks of fattened geese.

MY 1874 PHRENOLOGICAL ANALYSIS

Caroline Jukes

According to Professor O.S. Fowler
of Boston, Massachusetts,
I am unmistakably overtaxing

my brain and nervous system
and need my energies diverted.

I have a great amount of character,
am a resolute, efficient "go-ahead

girl," half-crazy half my time
with the wind of my desires.

I have a head unusually large
for a temperament so fine.

I am unusually smart
and would make a most excellent
teacher, physician, photographer,
designer, poet.

I am a prime speller, literally
forget nothing and speak

with perfect ease.

(Add: agreeable, lady-like,
prepossessing, courteous,
complimentary.)

Apparently, I would enjoy
myself in purgatory if I could

make those around me happy.

Intense in my affections,
I have a most loving nature

and an unusual amount
of the "womanly"

(all considered attributes
for a "complete wife").

I must marry a man who is:
wilful, smart, talented,
and above all, dignified

(I could not love a trifler).

Alas! Will Mr Gilbert Sanders
have anything to say?

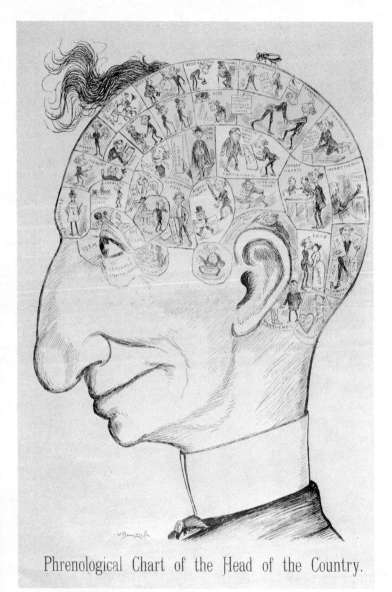

Phrenological Chart of the Head of the Country.

INDICTMENT FOR THE CRIME
OF HIGH TREASON

That Louis Riel
Not regarding the duty
of his allegiance

Nor having the fear
of God in his heart

But being moved
and seduced
by the instigation
of the devil

As a false traitor
against our said Lady
the Queen

Together with divers
other false traitors
armed and arrayed
in a war-like manner

Most wickedly
maliciously
and traitorously

did levy and make war
against our said Lady
the Queen

TESTIMONY: RIEL'S TRIAL

Augustus Jukes

I have seen him almost every day.
I would always speak to him in passing.

I have always watched him very carefully
so as to notice any appearance of unsoundness

of mind. I have seen nothing to make me question
his mental condition, and therefore have never led

the conversation, under any circumstances,
so as to draw out any possible insane notion.

I have never spoken to him on the subject of religion
and on his mission.

I never made a special examination of him as a lunatic
because my duty was otherwise.

Yes, it is so. You may converse with a man
continually and not be aware of his insanity

until you touch accidentally upon that point
upon which he is insane.

There are men who have held very remarkable views
with respect to religion, and who have been

always declared to be insane until they gathered
together great numbers of followers and became leaders.

The fact that a man might also labour under the insane
delusion that he had a mission would not necessarily imply

> *I have never spoken to him on the subject*
> *of religion and on his mission*

that he was otherwise insane or incompetent.
That would be my own judgment.

After a considerable amount of conversation
and daily communication with him,

I have never spoken to him on a single subject
on which he has spoken irrationally.

> *You may converse with a man continually*
> *and not be aware of his insanity*

I have never spoken to him specially with regard to
what he believes to be his mission. I regret to say that

> *until you touch accidentally upon that point*
> *upon which*
> *he is insane*

my hearing is rather imperfect in the court room.

RULES FOR POLITE TEA

Caroline Jukes

Officer wives clatter (their love for Royal Albert)
bone china all the way from London
      pink rosebuds set in white

The more experienced debate the risks
      of chokecherry jelly
      skin and seeds

A hint of lemon in the pound cake, please

Circulate the Montana story in hushed tones:
      farmer disembowelled in a field of corn
      blue-eyed child scooped up with the roan
      mother cut down in the seconds
            between clothesline
                  and kitchen door

No loosening of corsets
Contribute to the conversation
            in a thoughtful manner

*

I could mention the three boiled eggs
    my father brings to Riel
        on his morning rounds
        blue bowl steaming
            in the prisoner's cell
    Let them ponder hard   soft   cracked?

Or confess the soufflé practices
                each worsening collapse
                a sign of my own
                marriage prospects?

I could analyze the pink roses
on these perfectly balanced teacups
    Roses irritable from all that
        hauling up of skirts and elbowing of ribs
        to reach the cup's thin rim
        out of breath, ill-mannered
            teetering at the edge
        All for a grander view of the horizon

But in truth, for one good tight-lipped
look at their big-hipped country cousins
    Rosa arkansana
        sashaying pink across the prairie
        chasing invisible bison with garlands
        of themselves laced with *Stipa comata*

Ah, the last full-rumped romp before
the final ripping out and laying down
of civilized imported grasses
Bromus inermis
to please the civilized
imported cattle

I could hold out my girlish arms
forever, and never
witness a blue vein announcing
spirit (animal)
as the half-breeds are said to do

Brought Miss Ju_es home   *Gzqxhlt Rquv K_is mwoh*

Miss Ju_es in house   *Rquv K_is nv jrvwe*
but avoided me   *gcv dwsiimf pf*
I shall do same   *m smino es sfug*

Had quite a chat   *( ) ( ) ( ) hpcw*
with Miss Ju_es   *xmtm Ukot N_kx*

Felt spoony   *kmnw arrpry*
on Miss Ju_es   *tv oltw jzsgv*

Resolved to keep   *( ) ( ) ( )*
clear of Miss Ju_es   *htds sf RQUV K_is*
for a time   *lwt d ummj*

Men came from Winnipeg   to make up detachment
going north on account of   disturbances
I am not to go

Heard that I had to go   Had an explanation
with C.J. in afternoon

Started again at 6 p.m.   from Prince Albert
with 40 prisoners   (suspected rebels)
for Regina

Sgt McGibbon's horse   (No. 478)
dying, its tongue quite black   Prisoners slept
in open

Miss Ju_es birthday   *Rquv K_is gqtwihad*
Keep thinking of Carrie   *pmgs ulisskqh sf hituji*

xtgsu aivp Edsvij   Slept with Carrie (Huff)

Had some fun   in the evening
with other fellows   at *Gtcqdl's*

Sent my photo   to C.J.

Hogan's horse   (No. 571)
died this morning

Wrote a letter   to C.J.
this morning

Riel was hanged   this morning

Wrote Carrie and almost   *( ) Hituji asl conssy*
proposed to her   *xtrqssjl vr iir*

Started about 10 o'clock   with the Colonel
Cotton, Lord Boyle   and interpreter
for the Blood Reserve   Through some mistake
all the Indians were not   there, but a good many
amongst them   Red Crow the Chief

My birthday (22)
with house most
Felt like shooting

Had an awfully jolly

Christmas day. Stayed
of the time, read and slept
myself once or twice

letter from Carrie

T.W. Chalmers, Gilbert E. Sanders (standing), and J.O. Wilson (Glenbow Archives / NA-919-21)

FOUR CLOCKS IN THE TORONTO ASYLUM: NOTES ON DR DANIEL CLARK'S "MEDICAL EVIDENCE IN COURTS OF LAW"

Augustus Jukes

            This I know:
Take apart the clock and it is
no longer
        a clock.

Tamper with the smallest
        hinge
        that only
                the divine clockmaker knows
                and the whole being
                        falls asunder.

Many an insane person dies
and leaves
        no history
        of mischief in the head.
The medical witness must guard against
                being led into defining
                the insanity of the accused
                as being: want of power
                        to distinguish right from wrong.
        Many lunatics have that discrimination.

(1)

In the refractory ward
        a powerful mulatto
                        constantly persecuted
                with spirits
            and
                    intermittently
                            a longing to kill.
            At such times, he asks the supervisor
                        to lock him in his room.
        According to the law, should he
                commit homicide, he ought to
                            be hanged.

(2)

In another ward, a prominent writer
for the press, afflicted with chronic mania.
            On one occasion, he told Clark
                    he "felt like wanting to kill"
                            one of the patients
                    whom he disliked.
        He said he knew
                    it was wrong to think
                    so   and cunningly added:
                "You know I am crazy
                    so they wouldn't hang me."

(3)

She is an estimable lady
              afflicted
      with religious melancholy.
                    But she never loses her sense
                    of the wickedness of her
                    attempts.
        When the strong desire comes
                she begs to have
                the leather put on her hands
                        lest she accomplish
                              her design.

(4)

He had a firm step.
      He has now a   shuffling
                        gait.
He never decorated his person.
      He now makes a ring
      of some material
              for his finger   or button hole.
He was not a keen observer of small things.
      He now   notices
      and picks up
           pins
           nails
           screws
           bits of glass
           any small thing
               in   his   path
               placing them in some corner
                     in his pocket
          or elsewhere   on his clothing.
He may have had clear utterance.
      Now he has lost clear
           enunciation of words and *mumblesthemout.*

Since 18 June last, as many
        as eighty-one prisoners

        including lunatics
                (one of whom was female)

have been confined
        here at one time

*

Some suffered from milder forms
        of malarial disease
                (All ultimately recovered)

But a good deal of watchful
        attention was demanded by

                Riel, Jackson, and Parenteau

And by Connors, a condemned murderer
        who persistently feigned

        insanity.

HEADS MOUNTED ON WALLS

John Connors

I have joined a collection of Heads
mounted on walls, in separate cells

my well-appointed features gratefully
intact, skull scraped clean of cerebellum

but not of the unrehearsed
        finale: Enter scaffold (stage left)
        Cross to centre, et cetera
        Recite the Lord's Prayer
        Note to self: *And lead us not into temptation*
                      (cue for the hangman)

Consider, ladies and gentlemen
the role of the Severed Hands:
        The laying on
                of soft white cloths
                to silence Hysterical Mouths
        The pounding on walls
        if necessary. (The more
        sensitive Heads reverberate
                for hours
           sometimes days
        sometimes
                fall)

The Hands came to be severed
because they shot at everything that moved:
       mean-spirited thermometers
       in winter, Indians stealing the dogs'
       dinners, women with red hair

The birds soon grew wise to the perils
of one false note: one Fenian-hunting bounder
       whistling my name across Montana
       One bad joke (my own) about
       being in the wrong play

       or was it being
       in the battle
       without a costume?

I loved Eva –
an actress in my troupe

She saw meaning in morning
tea leaves, sang psalms
in Spanish before

       her graceful descent
       (they told me later)
       from the window

       of an unnamed hotel room
       of an unnamed constable –

       pants down, eye shocked
       from its socket, blood pooling
       on his newly issued Mountie boots

the carbine warm, chanting my
name, my inexplicable twitching
                                hand

At night I dream   I am floating out to sea
                on a glass-bottom boat
            Below, beneath the glass

            Eva: lovely bones
                flapping red mouth

She sings me *Yankee Doodle Dandy*
                in two-part harmony

DEAR MOTHER, PLEASE FIND ENCLOSED

Anonymous Constable

One clump of prairie soil
for Uncle John,

three arrow flints for cousin Peter,
one prairie chicken foot

for the taking, one photograph
of yours truly, considered

a fine specimen
of respectable manhood

who could have been
better than G.P. Arnold.

> (a dead shot, Arnold was:
> did not drink, pegged away
> at the enemy while
> wounded in the neck,
> until he was shot
> through the lungs,
>
> and that was,
> as they say,
> conclusive).

P.S. The recruiting officer led me
to believe I could buy out

the three-year term of my
engagement if I was not satisfied.

MORAL JUDGMENT

Augustus Jukes

Medical students did not consider
the aesthetics of the corpse
     pinned under the glare
     of amphitheatre light

No need to ponder a misaligned eye's
     skewed perspective
     of upper lip

We wielded the scalpel with clinical servitude
Sliced boldly toward the biology of lunacy revealed
     in inverse order:
       from moral judgment
       to intelligence to ideation
        to the bodily senses

*

      Not the hospital, je vous implore!

Isabella Stocks is twenty-two years old today
   Tomorrow, one hundred and five
The prisoners call her the Mad Filly
   Break her in Doc, she's up to no good

Each morning the same fierce
            grip on my sleeve
            wringing out nightly horrors:
                        mutilated corpses re-assembled
                        childhood lashings re-enacted
                                    with her own
                                    slim hand

                                    Je vous implore!

The guards fear her
            voice writhing through the cells
            urging men into prayer
            the rats to rise on haunches, sniffing
                        the promise of an earlier science

not this textbook summing up:
            the womb's innate instability
            the fatherless, the unmarried, the poor
            no manly hand to steady their nerves

    Not the hospital, je vous implore!

Some police horses are bound
            to escape at night, to break through
            young widows' fences to pound
            oat crops to smithereens

    Others dutifully haul water carts

No horse will face the flames unassisted
            To lead them out of fire
                        you must first blindfold them

JUST CALL ME THE FILLY FROM MOOSOMIN

Isabella Stocks

They prefer broncos, a native breed
purchased from a company whose name

escapes me. Saddle horses of strong
constitution. Docile and hardy. Able

to withstand these prairie hardships.
Myself? I prefer the harder bit, bleeding

in the corners of my mouth, the whip's
sweet song when gentlemen hold me down

so I'll shudder when the hot iron chisels
my flank (a valentine or someone's initials).

Oooh, the lilt of sonnets soaked in whiskey
gun-metal flash to my ear, old oats leeching

dust in the dark of a father's room, the house
roaring its Biblical rights as it crawls from flames

lit by the match of these – my averted eyes.
I imagine Selkirk Asylum in October:

the soft pink bellies of doctors, the guards'
handsome, broad-faced backs.

Augustus Jukes

The Blackfoot sixty years ago
numbered one hundred to one
of their present number

Then came the smallpox – *Sika-piksinn*
the third visitation (1869)

carrying away the remaining
two-thirds

In one camp, one hundred
tents of dead. Everywhere

the dead rolled up
in their buffalo robes

often in piles

*

> *Paint and dress his body as of old*
> *And lay it in the bed where we used to lie*
>
> *And lay me beside him*
> *and cover us up*
>
> *And leave us together*
> *as when in life*

*

She fastened a lariat to
the top of the lodge

An old ten-gallon keg
she pushed beneath it

She called in her husband's
relations, friends, the headmen

She said:

> *I love my husband*
> *I will go to him*
>
> *Let none try to prevent me*

Then she mounted the ten-gallon
put her head through the noose

and kicked the keg away

DEAR FATHER, I AM FEELING MUCH ENCOURAGED

Anonymous Constable

Despite hailstones the size
of Christmas puddings

Coyote's yellow eye, yip-yipping
after a charred left leg
(minus my feckless sock)

Items regretfully tossed
from my dead pony's pack:

Red woollen mittens from Mother
(or whomever it was she paid
to send her love)

Laura's "forever" locket
(mayflies ate her
portrait after she broke
with me)

Granny's recipe for mulberry
scones (I still don't read
Welsh)

I assume they presume
desertion. A little
whoop-up diversion

Not this perpetual
singing of the Blackfoot

dead in Cypress Hills

Mounties Fred Young and George B. Moffatt with Blackfoot (Kainai) man
(Glenbow Archives / NA-136-2)

MY SISTER'S RECIPE FOR "QUEEN PUDDING"

Caroline Jukes

½ pint of fine bread crumbs
½ cup of sugar
1 pint milk
yolks of 2 eggs beaten
grated rind of 1 lemon
a piece of butter ½ size
of an egg

Bake until done, but not
watery

Whip the whites
of the eggs with sugar
in which has been strained
the juice of 1 lemon

Spread over the pudding
a layer of jelly
Pour the whites
of the eggs over

this. Put into oven
to brown the top

To be eaten cold
with cream
if liked

*

I doubt even Her Majesty
could abide my sister's
(Mrs George B. Moffatt)

loopy mewling-wed
directions

ENDEAVOURING TO RESTORE ANIMATION

Augustus Jukes

The whole body, especially the head,
cold as ice, but unfrozen.

No perceptible pulse at the wrist.
Pupils insensible to light.

Teeth firmly clenched, as in locked
jaw. Head reared back – impossible

to bend – as in idiopathic tetanus
(produced by exposure and extreme cold).

The heart revealed a few feeble
pulsations, but many men being

about the bed, I had no certainty.
The rule in this country being:

Never begin a journey in a snowstorm.
Every landmark will be obscured.

Men left behind will become delirious –
the cold affecting the brain of ill-

protected heads. Hands strike out
at imaginary objects.

*

We applied frictions with hot
dry flannels, while endeavouring to excite

the respiratory muscles by means
of electricity. But after the most

energetic and assiduous application
for upwards of two hours,

not the slightest sign. I tried to
administer hot punch, but the power

of deflection was gone. I believe he was
dead when they brought him in

from the coulee on the trail to Maple Creek.
A stout, well-made man, about 21.

Richard Holt of London.

REMEMBERING ST CATHARINES PEACHES IN MASON JARS

Phoebe Jukes

I did not feel charitable in the morning
with all that carrying-on in the back room.

Such rude heaving against the calm
of yesterday's peaches still warm

in mason jars, dates inscribed at eye
level, reassuring about the day's precise

beginning and end. Twelve jars, no risk
of thirteen. Of excess procreation:

Forty-four harp strings sniveling
for a harp. Seven pillboxes lamenting

ill-fitting lids. Nine editions of *The Lady
of the Lake* reciting themselves hoarse.

Oh to purge all that clutter, let it clog
the new waterway, foul the morning

tea and servants' tempers over the mud
tracked in by coloured labourers wandering

up from the canal, wondering about safe haven
with all that carrying-on in the back room,

no distant aunt to hide a patient's shame, her
newborn bundled off at noon to nuns and a wet nurse.

The back room hot with sun. Ladybugs stupefied
in windowsill corners. Into my willing arms

she folded all of her thirteen years. Each
peach, a fist in the womb. Scent of a son

lost at sea.

The suspicion of a permit
caused the boys to hang

      around
      the Dominion Express Office
        and wait and
      wait and watch, until
  after a very long time
  the Express Company would be free
    to deliver the consignment.

Then there would be the gathering
and the wagon would be

    followed
    to its destination
      at a discreet distance
    by all the thirsty harpies
      who wanted to have a drink
        Sweet Jesus!
      at the expense
      of someone else.

If the owner happened to be away from home

        the visitors were out of luck

     but if, on the other hand

        he was there   *Sweet Jesus!*

      the crowd would follow

         the keg in

      and stay with it.

*

A Member of Parliament
on his visits to
his constituents in Edmonton

took with him a sleigh load

    of hog carcasses –

      pork bladders full

        of whiskey contraband

      no permits

     for such quantity smuggled in

    from Montana, the stuff known as:

Red Eye   Rot-Gut   Forty Rod

   and invariably

    of overproof

       (Sweet Jesus! Give me)

    strength

ON THE BEAUTY OF THE PASS

It is good for our Indians

No more having to explain
to them the terms

of the Vagrancy Act.

A pass for every occasion –
fishing, trapping, hunting, berry-

picking, shopping. Agents
shall report on

their movements.

If met with resistance,
simply threaten

to remove their names
from the rations list.

1 cup brown sugar
1 cup of ½ cream & ½ milk
1 tablespoonful of Golden syrup
½ lb. of English walnuts

IT WOULD BE WELL TO HAVE A SPY OR TWO

Hayter Reed

And to take away their ponies
Brand them
as our own

Take away their carts

No roaming about
without a pass

Now is the time
to strain every nerve

Gather the names
of those who have

misbehaved

Farm Instructors
to be charged

each time a vehicle
arrives from the reserve

improperly greased
or with breakages

WHAT MR PERCY ALLEN LOOKS LIKE

Phoebe Jukes

His feet shifting beneath the pew

His slight rocking to and fro

His wandering left eye

His balding head – speckled like a quail egg

His constant chewing

His explanations

The brown spittle on his chin

His soft humming

His dirty index finger

pressed to a horse's throat

Phoebe Jukes (Glenbow Archives / NA-2788-95)

FUTURE WRITING LESSONS

Isabella Stocks

I cannot imagine the good doctor
ever visiting Stony Mountain
Penitentiary empty-handed.

Surely he would bring proper
paper and writing utensils
to Big Bear and Poundmaker?

They could place a ledger pad
just so, in the slant of sunlight
on prison floor, the sharpened
pencils in single file.

He'd light his pipe and perhaps
suggest that they commence
with the letter "P" (*pledge,
peace, prosperity*) before

setting their hands
to the letter "Q".

INDIAN ACT 1876,
CHAPTER 18, SECTION 62

The Governor in Council
may order that the chiefs
of any band of Indians
shall be elected

for a period of three years
unless deposed
by the Governor

for dishonesty
intemperance
immorality
or incompetency

TOWARD A DEFINITION OF TREASON-FELONY, TRANSLATED FOR THE CREE

Alexander Morris to Chief Poundmaker:
>I see the Queen's councillors taking the Indian
>by the hand, saying we are brothers.
>We will lift you up, we will teach you
>the cunning of the white man.

Chief Poundmaker to Alexander Morris:
>From what I can hear and see now,
>I cannot understand that I shall be
>able to clothe my children and feed them
>as long as the sun shines and water runs.

Chief Big Bear to Louis Riel:
>We should not fight the Queen with guns.
>We should fight her with her own laws.

Edgar Dewdney:
>... any Indian being off his Reserve
>without special permission in writing
>from some authorized person,
>is liable to be arrested on suspicion
>of being a rebel and punished as such.

Court Interpreter to Chief One Arrow:
      (translation of translation)
           Knocking off the Queen's bonnet
           and stabbing her
        in the behind
           with the sword.

Chief One Arrow to Court Interpreter:
      Are you drunk?

NOTES ON BAND BEHAVIOUR DURING REBELLION

Loyal
A few impudent
Loyal
Four reported to have been North during the Rebellion
Names known
Awaiting trial
Loyal with one or two exceptions
Loyal
Very loyal
Name known. Not on pay sheets
Generally behaved very bad
Killed a large number of their cattle
Committed some depredations
Loyal – although several urgent appeals were made by Riel
Loyal
Loyal but very unsettled
Not deserving of special recognition
All disloyal
Ditto
Ditto
Should receive some mark of favour
Must be treated as Rebels
Reward these two Chiefs by giving them light waggons and
    horses
Disloyal
Disloyal

Disloyal
Took part in cattle stealing but not as armed rebels
Disloyal
Unsettled and should not receive any acknowledgment
Some raiding done
Loyal
Ditto
Ditto
Ditto
Ditto

REPORTING ON WHAT BIG BEAR SAID
AT HIS TRIAL

These people all lie.

They are saying that I tried
to steal the Great Mother's Hat.

How could I do that?

She lives very far
across the Stinking Water

and how could I go there
to steal her hat?

I don't want her hat
and did not know

she had one.

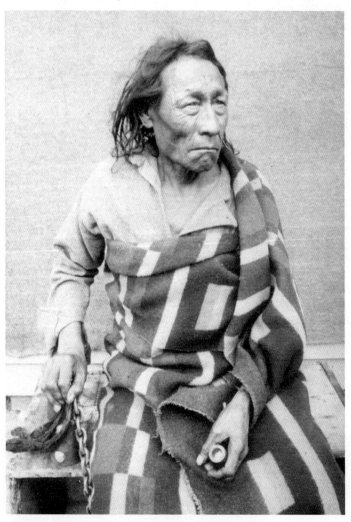

Big Bear / Mistahi maskwa (Photographer: Oliver Buell. Library
and Archives Canada / C-001873)

HOW TO HANG EIGHT INDIANS (AT ONCE) AT BATTLEFORD

Construct the gallows
twenty by eight

ten feet above   (*Sir John A. MacDonald,*
ground   *27 November 1885*)

Build a railing around
trap door. Test

          "*The executions*

(drop weights
simultaneously
from all the ropes)

Shave each head   *ought to teach*

Persuade one or two
to accept Christ

Ignore requests to be   *the Red Man*
shot; for shoes
with thick soles   *that*

Encourage the children
from the residential
school to attend   *the White Man*

Surround three sides
with 150 Mounties

                                          governs. "

Appoint four policemen
to escort each prisoner

in order:

Miserable Man /   *Kit-Ahwah-Ke-Ni*
Bad Arrow /   *Manichoos*
Round the Sky /   *Pah Pah-Me-Kee-Sick*
Wandering Spirit /   *Kah-Paypamahchukways*
Iron Body /   *Napaise*
Little Bear /   *Apischiskoos*
Crooked Leg /   *Itka*
Man Without Blood /   *Wawahanich*

Let them sing their songs

TEN STEPS TO L-U-N-A-T-I-C ON WALLS

John Connors

Taint a nun
      lain in attic

cut a "C"
      in ill-lit tit

lull a cat
      in nautical unit

nail in tail
      tuna in tin

tilt Aunt Una
      taut & anal

attain a Cain
      illicit clan

taunt a tunic
      annual antic

cull a cult
      call it tact

lilt a tic
        till a tactic

act a lunatic
        until actual

THE LUNACY COMMISSION

Sir Alexander Campbell, 23 October 1885

My dear Macdonald,

If it would get us over a fence, I would not at
all object to a private inquiry.

It is in England regulated by an act by which:

a Secretary of State,	upon alleged insanity
can authorize	an examination by
two surgeons or a	physician and a surgeon

If they find the prisoner	
insane, he is	committed to an asylum –
subject to being taken out	
and executed	if he be reported sane
at any time	

It would be safe enough to send Dr Lavell.
Lavell alone is what I would like.

A quiet inquiry and report
without loss of time,

no one to know.

Sir John A. Macdonald, 31 October 1885

My dear Lavell,

We desire that your trip and its object
should be kept a profound

secret. Dr Valade of Ottawa
will act with you in the examination

and report. I have told him that
as surgeon and warden of the Kingston

Penitentiary, you had under your charge
criminal lunatics and were therefore

an expert. I have fully impressed him
with this idea, so don't be too modest

about it. I would suggest speaking
to as few people as possible –

> so stop as soon
> as you are convinced

> that the prisoner knows
> right from wrong

> and is an accountable
> being.

*

Gentleman: Drs Lavell and Valade,

Representations have been made
        to the Government since Riel's
        conviction, that his mind

        has lately given way
        and that he is no longer

        accountable for his acts. I shall be

obliged by your immediate report
        of your opinions
        as to the accuracy

        of this representation. I need
        scarcely point out to you

        that the enquiry is not

as to whether he is subject
        to illusions or delusions,
        but whether he is

        so bereft of his reason
        as not to know

        right from wrong
        and as not to be

        an accountable being.

P.S.   I shall be obliged

by your telegraphing
your report in cypher.

Mr Dewdney
(who has a cypher
in me)

will enable you
to do so.

Edgar Dewdney, 6 November 1885

My Dear Sir John,

Your letters in regard to the visit
of the doctors reached me

today. I at once saw Dr Jukes
and will mail his independent

report tonight. He does not know
that any other medical men

are to examine Riel, but I will
tell him tomorrow. I fancy

there will be no mistaking
Jukes' ideas of Riel's

responsibility – but he
is against hanging

on general
principles.

Edgar Dewdney to Sir John A. Macdonald, 7 & 8 November 1885

Lavell arrived this morning
Jukes reverie, — — mangle
mailed last night, states:

Educates auspices trivial needy
Jukes report, which is long
medically — —, suitably:

refrigeration — affability
for his actions

Riel perfectly accountable
fungus ignore agnates

*

French doctor reports:

Generosity educate reveries:

ampliate hoof extremely chanced
Riel in private

After having examined carefully
refrigeration inevitably providential

cracknel timothy idly
and by testimony

conversation with him
aquiline carpentry transverse

overset plates George
take care of him

of persons who
tightly champagne overset idly

in hood concretely ultimatum
the conclusion that

I have come to
treated construe treads

hopping Kingfisher opiated
an accountable being

he is not
apprehensive affability blaspheme

treads hopping Kingfisher until
to distinguish between

that he is unable
ultimatum eagerly Bohemian

Morgan aquiline sachel padding
political and religious

wrong and right on
prefigured aquiline resource

tokens Cornelius in copperas
well marked typical

subjects which I consider
zinc metropolitan unsettling

galvanic overset acquaintability
kind of insanity

forms of a
laughed overset investigation

vanity Cornelius hopping
undoubtedly suffers

under which he
vegetable task

cargo padding paroquet predicated
I believe him to be

but on other points
in bleak idly ultimatum bide

recipe shunned aquiline
can distinguish

quite sensible and
caustic eagerly

sachel ghastliness Morgan

right from wrong

*

Penitentiary doctor reports:

Piebald educate reveries:

in aperture overset palatial treads
Riel, although holding

I am of opinion that
refrigeration, any imbiber

fumigation aquiline phase
views concerning visions

foolish and peculiar
whichevers conspire widenings

avenged ultimatum purport
and general government,

as to prophecy
aquiline grammaticize him,

Kingfisher apprehensive　　　　is an
accountable being　　　　　　　*affability blaspheme*

aquiline led　　　　　　　　　and knows
right from wrong　　　　　　　*sachel ghastliness Morgan*

*

There was a little difficulty about　the phraseology
between　　　　　　　　　　　the two doctors

which compelled them to send　　two separate reports.

Augustus Jukes, 9 November 1885

Dear Sir John Macdonald,

Having learned this afternoon
        that a short
        reprieve

        has been granted
        Riel

        I take the liberty of placing
        further information
        before you,

        which may serve to elucidate

        my too hastily written
        report of the 6th …

In view of the conflicting opinions
        expressed by greater
        or less recognized

        authorities, the question
        will hereafter

        be asked by many –

                was this man, after all,
                insane?

That question might be set at rest
            by a critical examination
            of his writings,

            and this would *precede*
                        his execution.

It is certainly possible
            that such an examination
            might reveal evidences

            of insanity. I have
            faith in my own
            opinion

            but an even greater
            regard for the truth

            and a desire
            that in this case,

the whole truth and nothing
            but the truth
            should be known.

Mistakes are possible to all,
            but should an examination
            of these papers,

            after Riel's execution,

            establish the fact
            that he was insane,

those whose evidence to the contrary
        had sent him
        to the gallows,

        however conscientiously
        they may have acted,

will have much to think of
        for the remainder
        of their lives

        with unavailing pain
        and regret.

Apothecary at NWMP barracks, Regina, Saskatchewan (Glenbow
Archives / NA-2435-1)

YOU'RE A PATIENT WOMAN, MRS JUKES

I did just like you instructed. I trailed him
real careful, he had no clue. I made sure
to stay downwind 'cause that Imogen,
she's got a keen nose and an even quicker

brain, which might explain your husband's
devotion. He don't suffer from delusions
from what I seen, but it don't take much
imagination to know what's expected:

Trade in that chestnut mare. Worse yet,
put her down at summer's end. *A liability*,
I heard the vet say, for a police horse
in the West. Too fine-boned, too delicate
a constitution to withstand harsh prairie

winters. You know about that
red flannel horse blanket your husband
stitched together? And them warm
bran mashes he sweetens with molasses?

I ask you: What kind of man
recites poetry to his horse?

Well, they don't go far. Just beyond
them trees – ten minutes if he lets her
canter. There's a pond – mostly a pudding
slick this time of year. She plods around

and around, and soon her legs are buckling,
she's found her spot. Your husband, he
leaps off just in time, removes the saddle,
bridle. And, whooeee! Down she goes! With
the biggest groan of pleasure. You ever?

Well, then. She rolls around, thrashes
the bejeebees out of them horsefly welts,
them nasty ticks and teensy eggs. Then she
springs to all fours, like she's been shocked
through with electricity, and the Doc's waiting

with a fresh bouquet. Hell, I don't know! Purple
clover? Sweet alfalfa? And Imogen's, she's
ambling toward him, all shy and girlish.
Lips fluttering. No, I didn't notice no

tremor in his right hand. He works
the curry comb real good, the mud
cracking, falling away. Then the soft
brush along the spine, down the flank –
you really want to hear all this?

A swollen tendon above the fetlock.
Right front leg. He lays his hands on,
closes his eyes. And it don't take much
imagination to know what must be done:

Single bullet. Right about here. No, I won't
take your money, Mrs Jukes. He saved
my baby girl, choking she was, turning blue.
But I gotta say this about your husband:

Something changed inside the Doc when
they done brought down that Louis Riel.

THE COMMISSIONER'S REPORT

To the Right Honorable Sir John A. MacDonald, G.C.B.
Sir: I have the honour to hand you my report for the year
1885.

PART 1

RECAPITULATION of cases tried and disposed of
in the North-West Territories during the past year:

High treason	7
Treason felony	92
Felony	12
Murder	17
Accessory to murder	4
Arson	4
Shooting with intent	2
Horse stealing	48
Bringing stolen property into Canada	1
Cattle stealing	9
Larceny	56
Embezzlement	2
Non-payment of wages	4
Selling intoxicants	29
Giving intoxicants to Indians	10
Intoxicants in possession	76
Manufacturing intoxicants	3

TO PUNISH

Augustus Jukes

In Latin, *punio*

Earlier, in Sanscrit, *pû* –

    (not mere striking

    not torturing

    not retribution

    not revenge)

Instead:

cleansing

correcting

delivering

from

the stain

a removal

*

He had always
told me that

he would speak
when led

to execution

but much to my
disappointment

he now declined

*

He remained
          hanging

for half
an hour

*

I shall not
mention

the blue
heron

     its dark
     head

     tilted

FOUR CLOCKS

(1)

In the Indian Department
     a powerful Comptroller
          constantly persecuted
          with money spirits
     and a relentless
          longing to slash
           expenditures.
    At such times, he travels to the West
          to witness starving
        Indians.
According to government policy, should he
       reduce food rations, he ought to
              be promoted.

(2)

In Regina, a prominent writer for
the *Regina Leader*, afflicted with himself.
    On the occasion of Riel's
          execution, he wrote about
          the beauty
           of the morning.
    He said he knew
          it was wrong to think
          so   and cunningly whispered:
         "You knew he was crazy
          but they needed to hang him!"

(3)

She is an estimable Queen
        afflicted
        with imperial reach.
            But she never loses her sense
            of the providence of her
            attempts
                at colonization.
      When the strong desire comes,
                she begs the commissioners
                to set their hands
                to another treaty.
      And the Indians hold her
                    to be
                        the Great Mother.

(4)

He had a firm vision.
        He now has a   railroad.
He never decorated his company.
        He now leads an entourage
        of carpet-baggers.
He was not a keen observer of small things.
        He now   notices
            and picks up
                Indians
                and half-breeds
                    in his path,
                    placing them
                    in some corner
                        of a
                        noose
                    or cell.
He may have had clear conscience.
        Now he is   stumbling about.

DICTIONARY

Augustus Jukes

Measles	*Aapikssinn*	(Blackfoot)
Tuberculosis	*Isttsikssaa-isskinaan*	(Blackfoot)
Smallpox	*Sika-piksinn*	(Blackfoot)
Whiskey	*Mniwakaska*	(Assiniboine)
White man	*Napikowann*	(Blackfoot)
White vandals	*Play-ku-tay*	(Assiniboine)
Buffalo/Bison	*Otapanihowin*	(Cree)
	Iniiksii	(Blackfoot)
Redcoats/Mounties	*Ii-moh-ksi-so-ka-sii-ksi*	(Blackfoot)
	Okne sha	(Assiniboine)
Promise/Sacred Vow	*Asotamâkêwin*	(Cree)
Indian Agent	*Kinnonna*	(Blackfoot)
	Shuniya o kimaw	(Assiniboine)
Poundmaker	*Pitikwahanapiwiyin*	(Cree)
Big Bear	*Mistahi maskwa*	(Cree)
One Arrow	*Kapeyakwaskonam*	(Cree)
Winter	*Sstoyii*	(Blackfoot)

ON THE DOUBLE SOURCES OF TYPHO-MALARIAL FEVER

Augustus Jukes

The first of these – malaria – abounds
in all the river bottoms during certain

seasons. The other source is animal
effluvia – from decaying bodies

and excretions passing into a condition
of putrescence – and generated where

considerable bodies of White men are
congregated for any length and where

cleanliness and intelligent observance of treaty
rules are not sanitarily enforced. By entrance

of this last into human bodies already
saturated with malaria, a mixed idiopathy

is generated, which depresses
the powers of life, corrupts

the blood and gives birth
to a complex moral disorder

in which the combined actions
of paludal and pythogenetic

influences unite in the production,
the fever varying in type as one Agent

or the other predominates, and too often,
of a very fatal character.

CONTAGION

Augustus Jukes

Laudable pus
Political speeches

This water
brought too late
to a boil

Lance and forceps
rattling
their pot

WHAT WATER LOOKS LIKE IN DREAMS

Augustus Jukes

Forced trajectory in the shining
spittoon ridding the system of not

white but not yet bloody path from
church a long black tongue extending

the brain the hand's drop the ink's
resolve gathering the eyes in floorboards

the soaking up the almost dead
the pennies dropped in

wells the swollen belly in the tepid
bath the empty pantry flask gun

barrel mouth eyes womb
the contaminated and the putrid

the skimmed-off rations the starved
Indians the dark stain spreading

on infirmary sheets the kitchen ceiling
the telegram to the Prime Minister

the priest's mark on the prisoner's
forehead the last swallow the last clink

in the scotch glass the ice breaking hooves
legs buckling the child's last singing

the missing chamber pot the washing
of bodies father mother seven children

the view from the bottom of the sea
the first ship crossing

Born in Bombay, India, Dr Augustus Jukes (1821–1905) was a physician, essayist, and poet. He practised medicine in St Catharines, Ontario, for thirty years prior to his appointment in 1882 as senior surgeon of the North-West Mounted Police (NWMP) in the Prairies (then called the North-West Territories). Stationed at Regina during the 1885 Rebellion, he played a reluctant role in Louis Riel's fate, beginning with his medical testimony at Riel's trial. He was appointed to a secret medical commission tasked with assessing whether Riel had become insane while incarcerated (and thus ineligible for execution). Three days after submitting his report, in which he declared Riel to be sane, Jukes wrote to the prime minister, requesting the creation of a new medical commission that would examine Riel's diaries for evidence of insanity. His request was ignored. Riel was executed a week later on 16 November 1885.

The Winter Count traces the deteriorating relations between First Nations and the government during this period, as told through a "cast" of speakers. Narrators include: Jukes, his wife Phoebe and daughter Caroline; Gilbert Sanders (NWMP inspector); Alexander Morris (treaty commissioner and lieutenant governor, NWT); First Nations chiefs Big Bear, Poundmaker, and One Arrow; Edgar Dewdney (Indian commissioner and lieutenant governor, NWT); Department of Indian Affairs bureaucrats Frederick White (Comptroller) and Hayter Reed (assistant Indian commissioner); Prime Minister Sir John A. Macdonald; Alexander Campbell (minister of justice and attorney general); and prisoners John Connors and Isabella Stocks.

The volume offers a collage of original and "found" poems, and sometimes hybrids of the two. Some lines are borrowed or adapted from various sources: annual reports of the NWMP, government correspondence, Aboriginal treaties, legislation, R. Burton Deane's memoir *Mounted Police Life in Canada* (1916), and the Jukes and Sanders families fonds held in the Glenbow Archives. Dr Daniel Clark's 1879 article "Medical Evidence in Courts of Law" is from the *American Journal of Insanity*. Chief Big Bear's trial statement is from *War in the West: Voices of the 1885 Rebellion* by Rudy Wiebe and Bob Beal (1985), and his speech is adapted from a longer version in Rudy Wiebe's *Big Bear* (2008). As well, I found inspiration in Blair Stonechild and Bill Waiser's *Loyal until Death: Indians and the North-West Rebellion* (1997), Candace Savage's *A Geography of Blood: Unearthing Memory from a Prairie Landscape* (2012), and Sarah Carter's *Lost Harvests: Prairie Indian Reserve Farmers and Government Policy* (1990).

I am grateful for grants from the Toronto Arts Council and Access Copyright Foundation, which assisted work on this manuscript. I thank the Glenbow Archives and Library and Archives Canada for assistance with research and for the use of archival images. Jim Johnstone published earlier versions of poems as a chapbook (*The Lunacy Commission*, Cactus Press, 2012). Anita Lahey edited early versions of *The Winter Count*. Sue MacLeod, Maureen Hynes, Ruth Roach Pierson, Jim Johnstone, and Daniel Scott Tysdal offered thoughtful comments. I thank Allan Hepburn for his incisive editorial suggestions. Edward, Oriana, and Brigid cheered me on, poem by poem. First Nations elder Cat Criger provided guidance. Augustus Jukes, my great-great-grandfather, kept my hand moving across the page. I dedicate this book to him.